A Rose for Your Pocket

A ROSE FOR YOUR POCKET

An Appreciation of Motherhood

THICH NHAT HANH

Parallax Press
Berkeley, California

Parallax Press
P.O. Box 7355
Berkeley, California 94707
www.parallax.org

Parallax Press is the publishing division
of Unified Buddhist Church, Inc.
© 2008 by Unified Buddhist Church.
All rights reserved.
Printed in the United States of America.

Cover design by Gopa & Ted2, Inc.
Text design by Jess Morphew.
Cover photograph by Helen Tadeo.

Library of Congress Cataloging-in-Publication Data

Nhat Hanh, Thich.
  A rose for your pocket : an appreciation of motherhood /
Thich Nhat Hanh.
    p. cm.
  ISBN 978-1-888375-80-0
  1. Motherhood--Religious aspects--Buddhism. 2. Mother
and child--Religious aspects--Buddhism. 3. Buddhism. I.
Title.
  BQ9800.T5392N45465 2008
  294.3'441--dc22

                                        2007044610

1 2 3 4 5 / 12 11 10 09 08

CONTENTS

INTRODUCTION

Betsy Rose

I first met Thich Nhat Hanh in 1987 at a retreat for artists in Ojai, California. From that first meeting, his teachings have permeated my heart and mind. When I first found Thay, as his students call him, I was in the midst of wrenching infertility struggles. His teachings on impermanence, nonattachment, suffering, and the causes of suffering, helped me to frame my experience in a different way, and hold the pain, effort, and loss a bit more lightly.

I gave birth to my son, Matt, in 1992. My practice was still very new and I was eager to be a perfect spiritual mother to my long-awaited child. Surely the equanimity, patience, and understanding that I developed on the meditation cushion would enable me to create the family of my dreams.

This confidence quickly disappeared. At eighteen months, Matt looked at me coolly, picked up my favorite teacup and smashed it on the sidewalk. Anger collided with grief over the broken cup, but more over my broken dreams for an easy, cooperative child. In preschool, his aggression and high activity level branded him the school hitter. As a Buddhist mom, I felt utter horror and shame at this public unmasking of my spiritual inadequacy as a parent. Throughout elementary school, I spent many sleepless hours contemplating the future, with recurring scenarios involving police, juvenile hall, and worse.

I have to say honestly that Thich Nhat Hanh's teachings did not make me the parent of a model Buddha-baby, nor was I constantly imbued with wise speech, equanimity, and mindfulness. Perhaps some readers will recognize themselves in this. Yet the loving and gentle wisdom contained in these pages, and in Thich Nhat Hanh's many other writings, have offered me something even better: acceptance of my, and my child's, humanity, compassion for both of our suffering, and a new way of seeing the inevitable disappointments, seeming failures, and sense of inadequacy that is our common lot as parents.

Thay is not only a poet, teacher, and peace-maker, but a gardener. His teachings on growing lettuce remind me that when a plant grows poorly, one does not scold the lettuce ("Bad lettuce! You could do better if you tried!"), but rather looks at the soil, the nutrients, the context that is feeding that lettuce, and adjusts what is lacking or toxic. This wisdom inspired me to change my child's school situation several times. It helped me look at what tensions and unexpressed negative feelings were present at home as clues to why he seemed inexplicably difficult. It increased my understanding of the causes and conditions that create all of our behaviors and moods. All this new soil did indeed yield a stronger, happier child.

Simply remembering to breathe, and to send a loving thought to my own heart in times of stress and anger, has prevented many a heated incident that I would have later regretted. Remembering the impermanence of his childhood, of the moments of unhappiness, and of the moments of joy as well, has created more patience for the hard times and less clinging to the good times.

And, as Thay beautifully expresses in this book, my own mother has become more real and present to me as I stumble along this path of mothering, facing the truth of my own failures, joys, and heartaches. My mother raised five children in the fifties and six-ties, before the feminist era, before society had any interest in or opportunity for her many other gifts besides mothering. As a young feminist, I judged her for her lack of assertiveness, her acceptance of a second place position in the marital structure. It is only as I live out my mothering years that I recog-nize her humor, stamina, enormous patience, and sly rebellions, too subtle to be noticed and squashed by the powers that be. My mother, too, grew in the soil given to her, with the heritage of her parents and ancestors. This awareness eases my tendency toward judgment and allows the beginning of true love and appreciation.

As Matt has grown through middle childhood and into his teen years, he has revealed himself to be a kind, deep, sensitive, and thoughtful human being. He is generous, quick to respond to injustice, and a loyal friend. Without taking direct credit for the mystery of how his, or my, Buddha nature emerges, I do believe that the seeds of kindness and peace and truth that we plant and water in our children benefit them and all beings.

Enjoy this little book of wisdom! It blossoms with sweetness, truth, insight, and clarity about the beautiful and complex relationships we live out in family life. May we all know peace and bring peace to those we love and to our world.

ONE

A Poem for Your Parents

Mother and father are called
"Brahma," "early teachers,"
and "worthy of adoration"
being compassionate towards
their family of children.
Therefore, the wise should pay
them due homage and honor,
provide them with food and drink,
with clothing and bedding,
anoint and bathe them
and wash their feet.
When he performs such services
for his mother and father,

that wise person is praised
here and now, and after death
he rejoices in heaven.

—Buddha, Itivuttaka 106

TWO

The Child's Palace

Do you remember anything from your stay in your mother's womb? All of us spent about nine months there. That's quite a long time. I believe that all of us had a chance to smile during that time. But who were we smiling at? When we're happy, there's a natural tendency to smile. I have seen people, especially children, smiling during their sleep.

No matter how hard our time is with our mothers once we are born, or whether or not they are the ones that raise us, for most of us, our time in our mothers' wombs was wonderful. We didn't have to worry about food or drink. We were protected from heat and cold. We didn't have to do homework or housework. Protected in our mothers' wombs, we felt quite safe. We didn't have to worry about anything. It's wonderful to have no worry at all.

I believe many of us still remember that time spent in our mothers' wombs. Many people have the impression that they were once in a safe and wonderful paradise and have now lost that paradise. We think somewhere out there is a beautiful place without worry or fear, and we long to get back there. In the Vietnamese language the word for uterus means "the child's palace." Paradise was inside of our mothers.

In the womb, your mother took care of you. She ate and drank for you. She breathed air for you, in and out. And I guess that she dreamed for you as well. I imagine you dreamed your mother's dreams. And if your mother smiled, I think you smiled too. If your mother dreamed about something difficult, and she cried in her dream, I guess that you probably cried with her. You shared her dreams and her nightmares, because you and your mother weren't two separate people. You were physically attached to your mother through the umbilical cord. And through that umbilical cord your mother channeled to you food and drink, oxygen, everything, including her love. You were there, you had not been born, and yet you were the object of love.

It is important to remember that you were nourished before you were born. If you look deeply, you will see that at the same time you also nourished your mother. Because of your presence in her body, her body changed and grew. She may have been more tired or not felt well, but at the same time, she may have smiled more and loved life even more.

Perhaps your mother talked to you before you were born. And I am convinced that you heard her talking with you and you responded. Perhaps it happened that occasionally she forgot you were there. So perhaps you gave her a kick to remind her. Your kick was a bell of mindfulness. If she was practicing mindfulness, she may have said, "Darling, I know you are there and I am very happy." This is the first mantra. Even if she did not say this or know this, her body responded, doing whatever it needed to so that you would be nourished.

When you were first born, someone cut your umbilical cord. Quite likely you cried aloud for the first time. Now you had to breathe for yourself. Now you had to get used to all the light surrounding you. Now you had to experience hunger for the first time. You were outside of your mother, but still somehow inside her. You were still dependent on her. You may have nursed at her breast. And although the cord was no longer whole between you, you were linked to your mother in a very concrete, intimate way.

As a baby, you know that you are linked to your mother, and as a mother, you can feel that you are linked to your child. If you are a mother, you may hold the view that you and the baby are one. But if you hold your baby and force it to be exactly like you, this is not correct either. It's good that you are one with your baby. But the baby receives other influences as well and, especially when the baby grows up, she could have new insights. Every mother has to learn to train herself to see that her baby, her child, is at the same time her but different from her. That child has her own life. You can't imprison your child and make her go in your direction and force her to do what you like because you want to shape her in your mould. Your child is not only the continuation of you, but the continuation of many generations of ancestors before you. Perhaps during your time you had no chance to water the good seeds you inherited, and so you don't have the same chance as your child. When your child has a lot of new insights, you have to learn from her.

If your mother had a hard time letting you be yourself, or if you are having a difficult time with your mother, you may fight very hard to convince yourself that you and your mother are two different people. But it's not really so. You are a continuation of both your parents. When I meditate, I can still see the cord connecting me to my mother. When I look deeply, I see there are umbilical cords linking me to other phenomena as well. The sun rises every morning. And thanks to the sun, we have heat and light. Without these things, we can't survive.

So one umbilical cord links you to the sun. Another umbilical cord links you to the clouds in the sky. If the clouds were not there, there would be no rain and no water to drink. Without clouds, there is no milk, no tea, no coffee, no ice cream, nothing. There is an umbilical cord linking you to the river; there is one linking you to the forest. If you continue meditating like this, you can see that you are linked to everything and everyone in the cosmos. Your life depends on everything else that exists—on other living beings, but also on plants, minerals, air, water, and earth.

Suppose you plant a kernel of corn and seven days later it sprouts and begins to take the form of a cornstalk. When the stalk grows high, you may not recognize it as the kernel you planted. But it wouldn't be true to say the kernel had died. With Buddha's eyes, you can still see the corn seed in the cornstalk. The stalk is the continuation of the kernel in the direction of the future, and the kernel is the continuation of the stalk in the direction of the past. They are not the same thing, but they are not completely separate either. You and your mother are not exactly the same person, but you aren't two different people either. This is the truth of interdependence. No one can be by oneself alone. In order to be, we have to *inter-be*.

When we are inside our mothers, there is no tension in our bodies. We are soft and flexible. But once we are out in the world, tension creeps in, sometimes from our first breath. Before we can release the tension in our bodies though, we have to release the tension in our breath. If our bodies are not peaceful, then our breath is not peaceful. When we generate the energy of mindfulness and embrace our breath, the quality of our in-breath and out-breath will improve. As we breathe in mindfulness, our breathing becomes calmer and more profound. The tension in our breathing dissipates. And when our breathing is relaxed, we can embrace our bodies and we can relax. The exact word that the Buddha used translates as "calm."

There is a Pali text called the Kayagatasati Sutta, the Contemplation of the Body in the Body. In it, the Buddha proposed an exercise for releasing the tension in each particular part of the body, and in the body as a whole. To begin, you can lie in a comfortable position and scan your whole body and then focus on different parts of the body. Begin with the head, or the hair on the head, and finish with the toes. You can say: "Breathing in, I am aware of my brain. Breathing out, I smile to my brain." Continue with the rest of your body. Like the farmer with his seeds, scan the body—not with x-rays but with the ray of mindfulness. Even fifteen minutes is enough to scan your body slowly with the energy of mindfulness.

When the fully conscious mind recognizes a part of the body and embraces it with the energy of mindfulness, that part of the body is finally allowed to relax and release its tension. This is why smiling is such a good way to help your body relax. Your first smiles in the womb were completely relaxed smiles. There are hundreds of muscles in your face, and when you get angry or fearful they get very tense. But if you know to breathe in and to be aware of them and to breathe out and smile to them, you can help these muscles release the tension. With one in-breath and out-breath, your face can transform. One smile can bring a miracle.

In the sutra on the Contemplation of the Body in the Body, the Buddha advises us to become aware of the four natural elements within the body. In the womb, these elements of water, fire, air, and earth are completely balanced. The mother balances the womb for the baby, sending in oxygen and nutrients as the baby rests in water. Once we are born, if we have a balance between the four elements, then we are in good health. But often these elements are out of balance; we cannot get warm or we find it difficult to take a full breath. Often, our mindful breath can naturally bring these elements into balance.

The Buddha also recommended that we become aware of our body's positions and actions. In sitting meditation, the first thing is to be aware that you are in a sitting position. Then, you can sit in a way that brings you calm, solidity, and well-being. In each moment we can notice the position of our body, whether we are sitting, walking, standing, or lying down. We can be aware of our actions, whether we are getting up, bending down, or putting on a jacket. Awareness brings us back to ourselves, and when we are fully mindful of our body and living in the here and now, we are in our true home.

Some of us did not feel at home in our parents' houses. Others don't feel comfortable in the world outside of the home. But each of us has a true home, as true and pure as that child's palace in our mothers' bodies. Even if you have the feeling that you don't belong to any land, to any country, to any geographical spot, to any cultural heritage, or to any particular ethnic group, you have a true home. When you were in your mother's body, you felt at home. Perhaps you long for a return to the place of peace and safety. But now, inside of your own body, you can come home.

Your true home is in the here and the now. It is not limited by time, space, nationality, or race. Your true home is not an abstract idea, it is something you can touch and live in every moment. With mindfulness and concentration, the energies of the Buddha, you can find your true home in the full relaxation of your mind and body in the present moment. No one can take it away from you. Other people can occupy your country, they can even put you in prison, but they cannot take away your true home and your freedom.

When we stop speaking and thinking and enjoy deeply our in- and out-breath, we are enjoying being in our true home and we can touch deeply the wonders of life. This is the path shown to us by the Buddha. When you breathe in, you bring all yourself together, body and mind; you become one. Equipped with that energy of mindfulness and concentration, you may take a step. And if you can take one mindful step, you can take another and another. You have the insight that this is your true home—you are alive, you are fully present, you are touching life as a reality. Your true home is a solid reality that you can touch with your feet, with your hands, and with your mind.

It is fundamental that you touch your true home and realize your true home in the here and the now. All of us have the seed of mindfulness and concentration in us. By taking a mindful breath or a mindful step, you can bring your mind back to your body. In your daily life, your body and mind often go in two different directions. You are in a state of distraction; mind in one place, body in another. Your body is putting on a coat but your mind is preoccupied, caught in the past or the future. But between your mind and your body there is something: your breath. And as soon as you go home to your breath and you breathe with awareness, your body and mind come together very quickly. While breathing in, you don't think of anything; you just focus your attention on your in-breath. You focus, you invest one hundred percent of yourself in your in-breath. You become your in-breath. There is a concentration on your in-breath that will make body and mind come together in just one moment. And suddenly you find yourself fully present, fully alive. There is no more longing to return to the womb, to your perfect paradise. You are already there, already home.

THREE

A Rose for Your Pocket

The thought "mother" cannot be separated from that of "love." Love is sweet, tender, and delicious. Without love, a child cannot flower and an adult cannot mature. Without love, we weaken and wither.

The one who raised you, loved you, and took care of you, you can call mother. For some of us, this was our biological mother. For others, it was an adopted mother, a grandparent, a guardian, or a friend. The day my mother died, I made this entry in my journal: "The greatest misfortune of my life has come!" Even an old person doesn't feel ready when he loses his mother. He too has the impression that he is not yet ripe, that he is suddenly alone. He feels as abandoned and unhappy as a young orphan.

All songs and poems praising motherhood are beautiful, effortlessly beautiful. Even songwriters and poets without much talent seem to pour their hearts into these works, and when they are recited or sung, the performers also seem deeply moved unless they have lost their mothers too early to even know what love for a mother is. Writings extolling the virtues of motherhood have existed since the beginning of time throughout the world.

When I was a child I heard a simple poem about losing your mother, and it is still very important for me. If your mother is still alive, you may feel tenderness for her each time you read this, fearing this distant yet inevitable event.

That year, although I was still very young,
my mother left me
and I realized that I was an orphan.
Everyone around me was crying.
I suffered in silence…

Allowing the tears to flow,
I felt my pain soften.
Evening enveloped Mother's tomb.
The pagoda bell rang sweetly.

I realized that to lose your mother
is to lose the whole universe.

We swim in a world of tender love for many years and, without even knowing it, we are quite happy there. Only after it is too late do we become aware of it.

People in the countryside do not understand the complicated language of city people. When people from the city say that mother is "a treasure of love," that is already too complex for them. Country people in Vietnam compare their mothers to the finest varieties of bananas or to honey, sweet rice, or sugar cane. They express their love in these simple and direct ways. For me, a mother is like a *ba huong* banana of the highest quality, like the best *nep mot* sweet rice, the most delicious *mia lau* sugar cane!

There are moments after a fever when you have a bitter, flat taste in your mouth and nothing tastes good. Only when your mother comes and tucks you in, gently pulls the covers over your chin, puts her hand on your burning forehead—is it really a hand, or is it the silk of heaven?—and gently whispers, "My poor darling!" do you feel restored, surrounded by the sweetness of maternal love.

Father's work is enormous, as huge as a mountain. Mother's devotion is overflowing, like water from a mountain spring. Maternal love is our first taste of love, the origin of all feelings of love. Our mother is the person who first teaches us love, the most important subject in life. Without my mother, I could never have known how to love. Thanks to her, I can love my neighbors. Thanks to her, I can love all living beings. Through her, I acquired my first notions of understanding and compassion. Mother is the foundation of all love, and many religious traditions recognize this and pay deep honor to a maternal figure, such as the Virgin Mary or the goddess Kuan Yin. An infant barely has to open her mouth to cry before her mother is already running to the cradle. Mother is a gentle and sweet spirit who makes unhappiness and worries disappear. When the word "mother" is uttered, already we feel our hearts overflowing with love. From love, the distance to belief and action is very short.

In the West, we celebrate Mother's Day in May. I am from the countryside of Vietnam and had never heard of this tradition. One day, I was visiting the Ginza district of Tokyo with the monk Thien An, and we were met outside a bookstore by several Japanese students who were friends of his. One discretely asked him a question, and then took a white carnation from her bag and pinned it on my robe. I was surprised and a little embarrassed. I had no idea what this gesture meant and I didn't dare ask. I tried to act natural, thinking this must be some local custom.

When they were finished talking (I don't speak Japanese), Thien An and I went into the bookstore and he told me that today was what is called Mother's Day. In Japan, if your mother is still alive, you wear a red flower on your pocket or your lapel, proud that you still have your mother. If she is no longer alive, you wear a white flower. I looked at the white flower on my robe and suddenly I felt so unhappy. I was as much an orphan as any other unhappy orphan; we orphans could no longer proudly wear red flowers in our buttonholes. Those who wear white flowers suffer, and their thoughts cannot avoid returning to their mothers. They cannot forget that she is no longer there. Those who wear red flowers are so happy, knowing their mothers are still alive. They can try to please her before she is gone and it is too late. I find this a beautiful custom. I propose that we do the same thing in Vietnam and in the West as well.

Mother is a boundless source of love, an inexhaustible treasure. But unfortunately, we sometimes forget. A mother is the most beautiful gift life offers us. Those of you who still have your mother near, please don't wait for her death to say, "My God, I have lived beside my mother all these years without ever looking closely at her. Just brief glances, a few words exchanged—asking for a little pocket money or one thing or another." You cuddle up to her to get warm, you sulk, you get angry with her. You only complicate her life, causing her to worry, undermining her health, making her go to sleep late and get up early. Many mothers die young because of their children. Throughout her life we expect her to cook, wash, and clean up after us, while we think only about our grades

32

and our careers. Our mothers no longer have time to look deeply at us, and we are too busy to look closely at them. Only when she is no longer there do we realize that we have never been conscious of having a mother.

In Vietnam, on the holiday of Ullambana we listen to stories and legends about the Bodhisattva Maudgalyayana and about filial love, the work of the father, the devotion of the mother, and the duty of the child. Everyone prays for the longevity of his or her parents, or if they are dead, for their rebirth in the heavenly Pure Land. We believe that a child without filial love is without worth. But filial devotion also arises from love itself. Without love, filial devotion is artificial. When love is present, that is enough, and there is no need to talk of obligation. To love your mother is enough. It is not a duty, it is completely natural, like drinking when you are thirsty. Every child must have a mother, and it is totally natural to love her. The mother loves her child, and the child loves his mother. The child needs his mother, and the mother needs her child. If the mother doesn't need her child, nor the child his mother, then this is not a mother, and this is not a child. It is a misuse of the words "mother" and "child."

When I was young, one of my teachers asked me, "What do you have to do when you love your mother?" I told him, "I must obey her, help her, take care of her when she is old, and pray for her, keeping the ancestral altar when she has disappeared forever behind the mountain." Now I know that the words "have to" in his question were superfluous. If you love your mother, you don't have to do anything. You love her; that is enough. To love your mother is not a question of morality or virtue.

Please do not think I have written this to give a lesson in morality. Loving your mother is a question of profit. A mother is like a spring of pure water, like the very finest sugar cane or honey, the best quality sweet rice. If you do not know how to profit from this, it is unfortunate for you. I simply want to bring this to your attention, to help you avoid one day complaining that there is nothing left in life for you. If a gift such as the presence of your own mother doesn't satisfy you, even if you are president of a large corporation or king of the universe, you probably will not be satisfied. I know that the Creator is not happy, for the Creator arises spontaneously and does not have the good fortune to have a mother.

I would like to tell a story. Please don't think that I am thoughtless. It could have been that my sister didn't marry, and I didn't become a monk. In any case, we both left our mother—one to lead a new life beside the man she loved, and the other to follow an ideal of life that he adored. The night my sister married, my mother worried about a thousand and one things and didn't even seem sad. But when we sat down at the table for some light refreshments while waiting for our in-laws to come for my sister, I saw that my mother hadn't eaten a bite. She said, "For eighteen years she has eaten with us and today is her last meal here before going to another family's home to take her meals." My sister cried, her head bowing barely above her plate, and she said, "Mama, I won't get married." But she married nonetheless. As for me, I left my mother to become a monk. To congratulate those who are firmly resolved to leave their families to become monks, one says that they are following the way of understanding, but I am not proud of it. I love my mother, but I also have an ideal, and to serve it I had to leave her—so much the worse for me.

In life, it is often necessary to make difficult choices. We cannot catch two fish at the same time, one in each hand. It is difficult, because if we accept growing up, we must accept suffering. I don't regret leaving my mother to become a monk, but I am sorry I had to make such a choice. I didn't have the chance to profit fully from this precious treasure. Each night I pray for my mother, but it is no longer possible for me to savor the excellent *ba huong* banana, the best quality *nep mot* sweet rice, and the delicious *mia lau* sugar cane. Please don't think that I am suggesting that you not follow your career and remain home at your mother's side. I have already said I do not want to give advice or lessons in morality. I only want to remind you that a mother is like a banana, like good rice, like honey, like sugar. She is tenderness, she is love; so you, my brothers and sisters, please do not forget her. Forgetting creates an immense loss and I hope you do not, either through ignorance or

36

through lack of attention, have to endure such a loss. I gladly put a red flower, a rose, on your lapel so that you will be happy. That is all.

If I could make a suggestion to those whose mothers are still living, it would be this: Tonight, when you return from school or work, or the next time you visit your mother, go into her room calmly, silently, with a smile, and sit down beside her. Without saying anything, make her stop working and look at her for a long time. Look at her well in order to see her well, in order to realize she is there, alive, sitting beside you. Then take her hand and ask her this short question, "Mother, do you know something?" She will be a little surprised and will ask you, smiling, "What, dear?" Continuing to look into her eyes with a serene smile, tell her, "Do you know that I love you?" Ask her without waiting for an answer. Even if you are thirty, forty years old or older, ask her simply because you are the child of your mother. Your mother and you will both be happy, conscious of living in eternal love. And tomorrow when she leaves you, you will not have any regrets.

This is the refrain I give you to sing today.

Brothers and sisters, please chant it, please sing it so you will not live in indifference or forgetfulness. This red rose, I have already placed it on your lapel. Please be happy.

FOUR

Reconciliation

Our feelings of love for our mother can also be mixed with feelings of anger and disappointment. The energy of mindfulness helps us to recognize our pain about our parents and embrace it tenderly like a mother whose baby is crying. When you were a baby, most likely the minute you cried, your mother stopped what she was doing and picked you up and held you tenderly in her arms. If your mother was not there to do this, someone else did. When we recognize and embrace the pain and sorrow within us, it calms down like the baby in her mother's arms.

Any rift with our parents is the same as a rift

within ourselves, because we are not separate from them. When we are calm, we recognize that there is always the chance for reconciliation, whether or not our parents are still living. Using deep listening and loving speech, we can heal any rift and at the same time heal ourselves.

The intention of deep listening and loving speech is to restore communication, because once communication is restored everything is possible, including peace and reconciliation. I have witnessed many couples practice deep listening and loving speech to heal difficult or broken relationships. Many fathers and sons, mothers and daughters, and husbands and wives have brought peace and happiness back to their families through this practice. With the practice of deep, compassionate listening and loving speech, they have reconciled.

During a retreat in Oldenberg, Germany, in the late nineties, after I gave instructions on deep listening and loving speech, four people left the lecture hall and immediately called their fathers. They practiced loving speech and listening deeply over the telephone. They had been estranged from their fathers for a long time with no communication, and they knew they could not let this continue any longer. They didn't need to go back home in order to do the work of reconciliation. They just called their fathers right away. The next day they told us they had been able to reconcile with their fathers using deep listening and loving speech. Listening to someone with compassion can turn him into a friend. It may be that no one else has been able to listen to that person; perhaps you are the first one capable of listening to him and giving him the relief he needs. You become a bodhisattva, a being who ends suffering. You lose an enemy and win a friend.

A young man came from America to visit us in Plum Village. One day he was asked to write down his mother's beautiful qualities. Other people were also given the assignment. Richard did not believe that he could write more than three lines. He said, "My father has many good qualities, but not my mother." However, he practiced like the others and, to his surprise, discovered after a few days that the list had grown quite long.

I think his mother had, at one time, made Richard suffer, and that suffering prevented him from seeing her other wonderful qualities. Let us think of the image of a dying tree. When you see one tree dying in your garden, you might think that all the trees are dying. This is not true. We don't see the trees that are still wonderfully alive. We are often caught up in our perceptions. This is not wise. We have to be objective and touch all aspects of reality. We mustn't allow one aspect to prevent us from seeing the whole picture.

With the support of the Sangha, Richard completed the exercise. Afterwards, as part of the assignment, he wrote his mother a very sweet, healing letter saying how proud he was to have a mother like her. Richard's wife told him that when his mother received the letter, she was incredibly moved. Richard had never talked to his mother with such loving words before. She had found a new son, born of the Dharma, full of understanding and love, and Richard had found a new mother. The new mother was born from Richard's deep looking. When he practiced deep looking, his true mother began to reveal herself to him.

His mother cried a lot after reading the letter. She told Richard's wife that she wished her own mother were alive so she could write a similar letter.

Richard was still practicing at Plum Village. When his wife told him this news, he wrote his mother another letter. "Mommy," he wrote, "don't think that Grandma no longer exists. She is still alive in you and in me. I can touch her any time I want, just like I can touch you. I am a continuation of Grandma and of you. So write the letter. Grandma will receive it right away and read it. You won't even have to post it." This is the insight he got from the teaching and from the practice, which corresponds to the deep teaching of the Buddha.

We all have to practice like that. Our presence here means the presence of all our ancestors. They are still alive in us. Every time we smile, all the generations of our ancestors, our children, and the generations to come—all of whom are within us—smile too. We practice not just for ourselves, but for everyone, and the stream of life continues. Richard's mother wrote a healing letter to her own mother. She cried tears of happiness while composing it. In the past, when her mother was alive, Richard's mother did not know the art of mindful living. Mother and daughter both made mistakes and created suffering for each other. Later, Richard's mother regretted this suffering and it became an obstacle to her happiness. Writing this letter removed that obstacle from her path.

If you have made mistakes and caused your beloved to suffer, and if he or she is no longer alive, don't be frustrated. You can still heal the wound within you. The person whom you think has passed away is still alive in you. You can make him or her smile. Suppose while your grandma was alive, you said something out of forgetfulness that made her unhappy and you still regret it. Sit down, breathe in and out mindfully, visualize your grandma sitting with you, and say, "Grandma, I am sorry. I will never again say anything like that to you or anyone else I love." If you are sincere, focused, and utterly mindful, you will see her smiling in you and the wound will be healed. Mistakes come from unskillfulness and forgetfulness, which are in the mind. Because everything comes from the mind, everything can be removed and transformed by the mind. That is the teaching of the Buddha.

Although we think the past is gone and the future is not yet here, if we look deeply we see that reality is more than that. The past exists in the guise of the present because the present is made from the past. In this teaching, if we establish ourselves firmly in the present and touch the present moment deeply, we also touch the past and have the power to repair it. That is a wonderful teaching and practice. We don't have to bear our wounds forever. We are all unmindful at times; we have made mistakes in the past. It does not mean that we have to always carry that guilt without transforming it. Touch the present deeply and you touch the past. Take care of the present and you can repair the past. The practice of beginning anew is a practice of the mind. Once you realize what mistake you made in the past, you are determined never to do it again. Then the wound is healed. It is a wonderful practice.

FIVE

*Ceremonies for Reconciliation
and Appreciation*

WALKING WITH YOUR PARENTS' FEET

When you walk, for whom do you walk? You can walk to get somewhere, but you can also walk as a kind of meditative offering. It's very nice to walk for your parents or for your grandparents who may not have known the practice of walking in mindfulness. Your ancestors may have spent their whole life without the chance to make peaceful, happy steps and establish themselves fully in the present moment. This is a great pity, but we do not need to repeat this situation.

All our ancestors and all future generations are present in us. Liberation is not an individual matter. As long as the ancestors in us are still suffering, we cannot be happy, and we will transmit that suffering to our children and their children.

Now is the time to liberate our ancestors and future generations: to free ourselves. If we can take one step freely and happily, touching the Earth mindfully, we can take one hundred. We do it for ourselves and for all previous and future generations. We all arrive at the same time and find peace and happiness together!

When you make a step, you may visualize that your mother is taking that step with you. This is not something difficult because you know that your feet are a continuation of the feet of your mother. As we practice looking deeply, we see the presence of our mother in every cell of our body. Our body is also a continuation of our mother's body. When you make a step, you may say, "Mother, walk with me." And suddenly you feel your mother in you walking with you. You may notice that during her lifetime she did not have much chance to walk in the here and the now and to enjoy touching the Earth like you. So suddenly compassion, love is born. And that is because you can see your mother walking with you—not as something imagined but as a reality. You can invite your father to walk with you. You may like to invite the people you love to walk with you in the here and the now. You can invite them and walk with them without the need for them to be physically present. We continue our ancestors, our ancestors are fully present in every cell of our body. When we take a peaceful step we know that all of our ancestors are taking that step with us. Millions of feet are making the same movement. With video techniques you can create that kind of image. Thousands of feet are making a step together. And of course your mind can do that. Your mind can see thousands and millions of your ancestors' feet are making a step together with you. That practice, using visualization, will shatter the idea, the feeling, that you are a separate self. You walk, and yet they walk.

It is possible for you to walk with the feet of your mother. Poor mother, she didn't have much opportunity to walk like this. You can say, "Mother, would you like to walk with me?" And then you walk with her, and your heart will fill with love. You free yourself and you free her at the same time, because it's true that your mother is in you, in every cell of your body. Your father is also fully present in every cell of your body. You can say, "Dad, would you like to join me?" Then suddenly you walk with the feet of your father. It's a joy. It's very rewarding. And I assure you that it's not difficult. You don't have to fight and struggle in order to do it. Just become aware, and everything will go well.

You may also like to sit for your mother. Many mothers don't get many opportunities to sit down and do nothing. This is important work! You can sit and just breathe mindfully, and this will be something you can do for your mother, whether she has passed on or is still with you, whether she is far away or near.

After you have been able to walk for your dear ones, you can walk for the people who have made your life miserable. You can walk for those who have attacked you, who have destroyed your home, your country, and your people. These people weren't happy. They didn't have enough love for themselves and for other people. They have made your life miserable and the life of your family and your people miserable. And there will be a time when you'll be able to walk for them too. Walking like that, you become a Buddha, you become a bodhisattva filled with love, understanding, and compassion.

THE FIRST EARTH-TOUCHING

In the Buddhist tradition I am part of, we do a practice called "Touching the Earth" every day. It helps us in many ways. You too could be helped by doing this practice. When you feel restless or lack confidence in yourself, or when you feel angry or unhappy, you can kneel down and touch the ground deeply with your hand. Touch the Earth as if it were your favorite thing or your best friend.

The Earth has been there for a long time. She is mother to all of us. She knows everything. The Buddha asked the Earth to be his witness by touching her with his hand when he had some doubt and fear before his awakening. The Earth appeared to him as a beautiful mother. In her arms she carried flowers and fruit, birds and butterflies, and many different animals, and offered them to the Buddha. The Buddha's doubts and fears instantly disappeared.

Whenever you feel unhappy, come to the Earth and ask for her help. Touch her deeply, the way the Buddha did. Suddenly, you too will see

52

the Earth with all her flowers and fruit, trees and birds, animals and all the living beings that she has produced. All these things she offers to you.

You have more opportunities to be happy than you ever thought. The Earth shows her love to you and her patience. The Earth is very patient. She sees you suffer, she helps you, she protects you. When we die, she takes us back into her arms.

With the Earth you are very safe. She is always there, in all her wonderful expressions like trees, flowers, butterflies, and sunshine. Whenever you are tired or unhappy, Touching the Earth is a very good practice to heal you and restore your joy.

Where I live, in Plum Village, we have a practice called the Five Earth-Touchings, and we begin by bowing down to our parents and ancestors. Touching the Earth helps us return to our roots and to recognize that we are not alone but connected to a whole stream of spiritual and blood ancestors. We touch the Earth to let go of the idea that we are separate and to remind ourselves that we are the Earth and part of life.

To begin this practice, join your palms in front of your chest in the shape of a lotus bud. Then gently lower yourself to the ground so that all four limbs (forearms and shins) and your forehead are resting comfortably on the floor. (If it's more comfortable, you can lie with your body extended flat on the floor or you can remain sitting or standing with your palms joined.) While in the Earth-Touching position, turn your palms face up, showing your openness to the Three Jewels: the Buddha, Dharma, and Sangha. Breathe in all the strength and stability of the Earth, and breathe out to release your clinging to any suffering. This is a wonderful practice, deepening our aspiration to live an awakened life in peace and harmony with ourselves and others, and healing the wounds that lie buried within our bodies and minds. We can practice Touching the Earth by ourselves or together with others, appointing one person to read the words aloud:

> I see my mother and father, whose blood, flesh, and vitality are circulating in my own veins and nourishing every cell in me. Through them, I see my four grandparents. Their expectations, experiences, and wisdom have been transmitted from so many generations of ancestors. I carry in me the

life, blood, experience, wisdom, happiness, and sorrow of all generations. The suffering and all the elements that need to be transformed, I am practicing to transform. I open my heart, flesh, and bones to receive the energy of insight, love, and experience transmitted to me by all my ancestors. I see my roots in my father, mother, grandfathers, grandmothers, and all my ancestors. I know I am only the continuation of this ancestral lineage. Please support, protect, and transmit to me your energy. I know wherever children and grandchildren are, ancestors are there also. I know that parents always love and support their children and grandchildren, although they are not always able to express it skillfully because of difficulties they themselves encountered. I see that my ancestors tried to build a way of life based on gratitude, joy, confidence, respect, and loving kindness. As a continuation of my ancestors, I bow deeply and allow their energy to flow through me. I ask my ancestors for their support, protection, and strength.

WRITING A LOVE LETTER

We can write a letter in which we water the flowers in our parents or children. We can water their positive seeds of happiness, loving kindness, forgiveness, and joy. We call this the practice of selective watering. We water the flowers, not the garbage, so that the flowers will bloom in the other person. When we make the other person smile, we benefit as well. It doesn't take long to see the result of our practice. She can smile because you have helped her to be happy.

If we love someone, we can practice this. It's not difficult to look into a person and recognize the positive seeds that exist in every one of us. Happiness is not an individual matter. The happiness of our parents and our children brings us happiness. That is why we practice. We bring back the smile to our loved one's face. We can do it. We have lived with her for a long time and know her weaknesses, strengths, and positive seeds. Why hesitate?

If you have difficulties with a parent or a

child, you might spend some time alone and write a letter to him or her. Give yourself three hours to write a letter using loving speech. While you write the letter, practice looking deeply into the nature of your relationship. Why has communication been difficult? Why has happiness not been possible? You may want to begin like this:

"My dear son [or daughter or mother or father], I know you have suffered a lot during the past many years. I have not been able to help you—in fact, I have made the situation worse. It is not my intention to make you suffer. Maybe I am not skillful enough. Maybe I try to impose my ideas on you and I make you suffer. In the past I thought you made me suffer, that my suffering was caused by you. Now I realize that I have been responsible for my own suffering, and I have made you suffer. As your father I don't want you to suffer. Please help me. Please tell me of my unskillfulness in the past so that I will not continue to make you suffer, because if you suffer I will suffer too. I need your help, my dear son [or daughter or mother or father].

"We should be a happy parent and child. I am determined to make this the reality. Please tell me what is in your heart. I promise to do my best to refrain from saying things or doing things that make you suffer. You need to help me, otherwise it's not possible for me to do it. I can't do it alone. In the past, every time I suffered I was inclined to punish you and say or do things that made you suffer. I thought that was the way to get relief, but I was wrong. I realize now that anything I say or do that makes you suffer makes me suffer also. I am determined not to do it anymore. Please help me."

Spend three hours, even a day, writing such a letter. You will find that the person who finishes the letter is not the same person who began it. Peace, understanding, and compassion have transformed you. A miracle can be achieved in twenty-four hours. That is the practice of loving speech.

HUGGING MEDITATION

Intellectually, we may know that things are impermanent, but we tend to behave as if the things and people in our life were permanent. If we can train ourselves to maintain the insight of impermanence every minute of our lives, then we will always have wisdom and happiness.

We all feel insecure. We don't know what the future holds. Accidents happen. A loved one may suddenly be struck by an incurable disease and die. We are not sure if we'll be alive tomorrow. This is all part of impermanence. This feeling of insecurity makes us suffer. How can we face this feeling? What is our practice? I think living deeply in the present moment is what we have to learn and practice to face this feeling of insecurity. We have to handle the present moment well. We live deeply in the present moment so that in the future we will have no regrets. We are aware that we and the person in front of us are both alive. We cherish the moment and do whatever we can to make life meaningful and to make him happy in this moment.

I propose hugging meditation for when we are angry with someone in our family—and also for when we're not angry! We close our eyes, take a deep breath, and visualize ourselves and our beloved three hundred years from now. Then, the only meaningful thing to do is to open our arms and hug him. When you hug someone, first practice breathing in and breathing out to bring your insight of impermanence to life. "Breathing in, I know that life is precious in this moment. Breathing out, I cherish this moment of life." You smile at the person in front of you, expressing your desire to hold him in your arms. This is a practice and a ritual. When you bring your body and mind together to produce your total presence, to become full of life, it is a ritual.

When I drink a glass of water, I invest one hundred percent of myself in drinking it. You should train yourself to live every moment of your daily life like that. Hugging is a deep practice. You need to be totally present to do it correctly. When you open your arms and hold the other person, you practice three mindful breaths. "Breathing in, I know that he is still alive in my arms. Breathing out, I feel so happy."

Life becomes real at that moment. Architects

need to build airports and railway stations so that there is enough room to practice hugging. You can also practice it in the following way: during the first in-breath and out-breath, you become aware that you and your beloved are both alive; for the second in-breath and out-breath, you think of where you will both be three hundred years from now; and for the third in-breath and out-breath, you go back to the insight that you are both alive. Your hugging will be deeper, and so will your happiness.

About the Authors

THICH NHAT HANH was born near Hue in Central Vietnam. At sixteen, he became a novice monk. During the Vietnam war, he founded the School of Youth for Social Service (SYSS) where he trained young people as social workers to help with rebuilding villages and sheltering refugees. For these activities, he was exiled to France. During a speaking tour of North America, he met Thomas Merton and Dr. Martin Luther King, Jr., who nominated him for the Noble Peace Prize. In 1969, Nhat Hanh led the Buddhist Peace Delegation to the Paris Peace Accords. In 1982, he founded Plum Village, a monastery and practice center in southwest France where he continues to live and teach. Thay ("teacher"), as he is known to his students and friends, travels around the world giving talks and leading retreats. He has taught at Columbia, Cornell, and the Sorbonne. In 2005, after nearly forty years in exile, he returned to visit Vietnam.

BETSY ROSE is a singer and songwriter, mother, and peace activist. She has written and recorded songs based on the poetry and teachings of Thich Nhat Hanh, and is co-leader of the Family Practice program at Spirit Rock Meditation Center. She leads community singing events for women, children, and groups working for peace and justice. Her recording, *Calm Down Boogie* brings simple teachings on breath, mindfulness, and simplicity to children and families. She lives in Berkeley, California with partner David Stark and her son Matthew.

Parallax Press, a nonprofit organization, publishes books on engaged Buddhism and the practice of mindfulness by Thich Nhat Hanh and other authors. All of Thich Nhat Hanh's work is available at our online store and in our free catalog. For a copy of the catalog, please contact:

Parallax Press
P.O. Box 7355
Berkeley, CA 94707
Tel: (510) 525-0101
www.parallax.org

Monastics and laypeople practice the art of mindful living in the tradition of Thich Nhat Hanh at retreat communities in France and the United States. To reach any of these communities, or for information about individuals and families joining for a practice period, please contact:

Plum Village
13 Martineau
33580 Dieulivol, France
info@plumvillage.org

Blue Cliff Monastery
3 Mindfulness Road
Pine Bush, NY 12566
www.bluecliffmonastery.org

Deer Park Monastery
2499 Melru Lane
Escondido, CA 92026
deerpark@plumvillage.org

For a worldwide directory of Sanghas practicing in the tradition of Thich Nhat Hanh, please visit **www.iamhome.org**.